DAI LARFIN'S WORST JOKES

What do you give a drowned rodent?
Mouse to mouse resuscitation.

When does a teacher need dark glasses?
When she has bright pupils.

A great collection of super jokes to give you the
reputation for being the greatest story-teller around,
collected by Tommy Boyd.

DAI LARFIN'S
WORST JOKES

by
Tommy Boyd

Hippo Books
Scholastic Publications Ltd
London

Scholastic Publications Ltd, 141-143 Drury Lane,
London WC2B 5TG, England

Scholastic Book Services, 50 West 44th Street,
New York, NY 10036, USA

Scholastic Tab Publications Ltd, 123 Newkirk Road,
Richmond Hill, Ontario L4C 3G5, Canada

Ashton Scholastic Pty Ltd, Box 579, Gosford,
New South Wales, Australia

Ashton Scholastic Ltd, 9-11 Fairfax Avenue, Penrose,
Auckland, New Zealand

First published by Scholastic Publications Ltd 1982
Copyright © Tommy Boyd 1982
Illustrations copyright © Steven Smallman 1982
All rights reserved

Made and printed in Great Britain
by Cox & Wyman Ltd, Reading

Set in Palatino by Input Typesetting Ltd, London SW19 8DR

CONTENTS

Have you noticed that the urge to giggle uncontrollably always comes over you at the most embarrassing moments? Practically everyone has dissolved into fits of stifled laughter at the back of the class, or during a church service . . . and wished they could die. It often happens to people on television or on the stage and when it does they call it "corpsing". I really wanted to get this into the title of the book somewhere, but the publishers said no one would understand it, so I thought a word of explanation would help.

When I played Dai Larfin on the BBC award-winning programme Jigsaw, it happened quite often! Dai was the super-villain who tried to take over the world by telling so many jokes that everyone was helpless with mirth. His plan backfired when he heard the world's worst joke and literally dissolved. He isn't here now, but he left behind some of his favourite jokes to be getting on with. I haven't included the "worst joke in the world", as I would hate to see all of you disappear too!

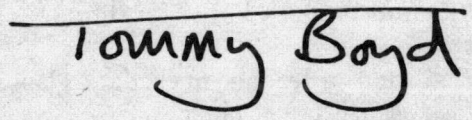

1 Skool rules . . .

When is a teacher like a bull?
When he's in charge.

Why did the dunce take a ladder to class?
Because he wanted to go to High School.

Why did the dunce take a sledgehammer to school?
Because it was breaking-up day.

Teacher: "Now, Dicky, how far is it to Pakistan?"
Clever Dicky: "Dunno miss, but it can't be far. My mate, Mushtaq, comes from Pakistan and he goes home for dinner."

When does a teacher need dark glasses?
When she has bright pupils.

Where do parrots learn to talk?
At a polytechnic.

Who's... a... pretty... boy...

Teacher: "Now, Norman, if I borrow £10 from your father and pay him back £1 per month, at the end of six months how much will I owe him?"
Norman: "£10 miss."
Teacher: "I'm afraid you don't know much about maths, boy."
Norman: "I'm afraid you don't know much about my dad, miss."

Teacher had been telling the class all about France.
Teacher: "So, Charlie, would you like to have been born in France?"
Charlie: "No, miss."
Teacher: "Why on earth not?"
Charlie: "Because I can't speak French."

9

. . . and if anybody ever asks you these questions:

Who wrote "Great Eggspectations"?
Charles Chickens.

Where is Felixstowe?
At the end of his foot.

Where do tadpoles change into frogs?
In the croakroom.

Where would you find the Andes?
At the end of the wristies.

Clever Dicky: "I wish I'd lived in ancient times."
Teacher: "Why?"
Clever Dicky: 'Then I wouldn't have had to learn history."

Dad: "Richard, how are your marks at school?"
Richard: "They're underwater."
Dad: "Underwater?"
Richard: "Yes. They're all below C."

. . . sometimes the teacher gets the better of Dicky.
Clever Dicky: "Please miss, what's the best way to become a mountaineer?"
Teacher: "You start at the bottom and work your way up."

2   Sport on Two

One football fan to another: "Are you going to see United on Saturday?"

"No, they never come to see me when I'm sick."

Which footballer is the most troublesome?
The centre-forward . . . he's a striker.

Why is it always cold at football matches?
Because of all the fans.

What's silver, has coloured ribbons, and snores?
The F.A. Kip.

Two flies were playing football in a saucer. One said to the other, "You'd better pull your socks up, we're playing in the cup next week."

Why is Cinderella a rotten footballer?
Because she has a pumpkin for a coach.

Have you heard about the world's worst goal-keeper? He became so depressed he decided to throw himself under a bus. It didn't work though. The bus just slipped under his body.

One football fan to another: "I'd like to be a football manager when I grow up."
"Really, why?"
"Because I like to keep on the move."

During a jungle football match the elephant stamped on the mouse, squashing him flat. "Foul," cried the referee. "I'm sending you off for that!"
"I'm sorry, ref," the elephant replied, "I was only trying to trip him."

Which Caribbean cricket team play dressed only in their underwear?
The Vest Undies.

Why are cricketers cowards?
Because they are afraid of a duck.

What is a horse's favourite sport?
Stable tennis.

What sort of a party do golfers like?
A tee-party!

The vicar had become a real golf fanatic. So much so that when he woke very early one Sunday morning and saw that the sun was shining, he couldn't resist the temptation to play a round, even though it was the day of rest. He'd managed to get halfway round the course without anyone spotting him, and was feeling very pleased with himself. However, up in heaven, God was watching. He called over the Archangel

Gabriel. "That vicar needs to be taught a lesson," he said.

"What are you going to do?" asked Gabriel.

"Watch this," said God.

Down below the vicar was about to play a tee shot on the most difficult hole on the course. He swung the club, made perfect contact, and watched in amazement as the ball flew high and true towards the green, where it bounced twice before rolling obediently into the hole.

"A hole in one?" asked Gabriel. "I thought you were going to punish him."

"I have," said God. "Who is he going to be able to tell?"

3 Relatively Speaking

What do you get if you cross a granny with an anorak?
A nanny coat.

What do you get if you cross a granny with an owl?
A hootnanny.

What do you get if you cross a granny with an ice-cream parlour?
A hot ba-nanny split.

What is elderly, and grey, and is lodged halfway up a cliff?
A rock cranny.

How do you make anti-freeze?
Stick her in the fridge!

4 Food for Thought

What sort of snack do fighter pilots prefer?
Scrambled eggs.

What sort of breakfast do comedians prefer?
Cornflakes.

What sort of breakfast do birds prefer?
Shredded tweet.

What sort of meat do Karate experts prefer?
Chops.

What sort of fish do cobblers prefer?
Sole.

What sort of vegetables do athletes prefer?
Runner beans.

What sort of vegetables do watchmakers prefer?
Spring greens.

"Waiter, waiter, there's a twig in my soup."
"I'm not surprised, sir, we have branches everywhere."

"Waiter, waiter, this coffee tastes like mud."
"I'm not surprised, sir, it was only ground this morning."

"Waiter, waiter, have you got frogs legs?"
"Yes, sir."
"Well, hop off and get me a sandwich."

"Waiter, waiter, have you got a wine list."
"No sir, it's just that one leg is shorter than the other."

"Waiter, waiter. Fetch me an alligator sandwich, and make it snappy."

What goes round the kitchen at 600 kph?
An unidentified flying omelette.

Who owns all the milk in Saudi Arabia?
A milk sheik.

What is a barbecue?
A queue of men waiting for a haircut.

5 History repeats itself . . . itself . . . itself

Who was Russia's greatest gardener?
Ivan-hoe.

Which famous chiropodist ruled England?
William the Corn-curer.

Who conquered half the world, laying eggs along the way?
Attila the hen.

Who did not invent the aeroplane?
The Wrong brothers.

Which cyclist defeated the Armada?
Sir Francis Trike.

Who was the thinnest Emperor?
Napoleon Boneypart.

Who was the noisiest hero of all time?
Gungha Din.

What is full of hay and conquered
Mongolia?
Genghis Barn.

Which king was fond of chestnuts?
William the Conkerer.

Who was round and purple and ruled
Russia?
Peter the Grape.

6 Hee haws!

What's fat, lives in mud, and goes up the front of anoraks?
A zipperpotamus.

Which subject do insects prefer at school?
Mothematics.

What would a grizzly bear do at school?
Anything he felt like.

What's grey and flies out of a burrow at 200 kph?
A hareoplane.

What sort of fish would make good newsreaders?
Topical fish.

Where do big black birds go to enjoy a drink?
A crowbar.

What do you give a drowned rodent?
Mouse to mouse resuscitation.

Which animal should you take on a day
out in the country?
A picnic hamster.

What is an artist's favourite animal?
A sketching weasel.

What's small and furry, and cuts corn?
A combine hamster.

What do you call a cat with eight legs?
An octopussy.

First boy: "I've lost my dog. What should I do?"
Second boy: "Put an advertisement in the paper."
First boy: "No point, he can't read."

Mother: "Have you put fresh water in the goldfish bowl?"
Son: "No point, Mum, they haven't drunk the last lot yet."

First boy: "I've lost my budgie. What should I do?"
Second boy: "Tell the Flying Squad."

First boy: "Why is your dog called 'Blacksmith'?"
Second boy: "Because every time I come in he makes a bolt for the door."

First boy: "I've just been bitten by a dog!"
Second boy: "Did you put anything on it?"
First boy: "No. He seemed to like it just as it was."

Where do baby apes sleep?
In apricots.

What did the two horses want in the theatre?
A couple of stalls.

Why did the Romans build straight roads?
Because they didn't want to drive their horses round the bend.

What sort of animal would make a good cook?
A grilla.

Why do cows wear bells?
Because their horns don't work.

How does a cat go up the M1?
Meeeeeeeeeeeooooooooooow.

How do ducks dance?
Slow, slow, quack, quack, slow.

Why was the sheep arrested in the High Street?
For doing a ewe-turn.

What should you do if there's an elephant chasing you?
Make a trunk-call and reverse the charge.

What do you get if you put a flock of ducks in a crate?
A box of quackers.

Why are woodpeckers bad company?
Because they are always boring.

What weighs two-and-a-half tonnes and squeaks?
A hippopotamouse.

7 It makes you laugh

One of the members of a very fierce tribe of cannibals was setting out from the village for a day's hunting when his wife called out to him: "Make sure you bring back something different today. The children are getting tired of the same old food."

"Yes, dear," said the hunter, and loped off into the jungle.

It was a long, hot day, and as the sun began to set, the hunter still hadn't caught anything. He was just beginning to worry about what his wife would say, when he came across a clearing in the jungle in which a terrible battle was taking place. A huge boa constrictor was wrestling with a tiny native man. Creeping up behind them the hunter knocked them both out cold, squeezed them into his bag, and set off back to the village. When he returned his wife was waiting for him.

"Well?" she demanded. "What have you got for tea tonight?"

"You're lucky I managed to get anything at all," replied the hunter. "But go ahead and take a look anyway."

The wife grabbed his bag, opened it up and stared at the contents.

"Oh, no!!" she exclaimed. "Not snake and pygmy pie AGAIN!"

A man and his wife arrived at Heathrow after a long and difficult journey from Plymouth. As their flight was announced, the man turned to his wife and said: "I do wish I'd brought the piano with us."

"What on earth for?" asked his puzzled wife.

"Because," replied the man, "I've left the tickets on it."

A man went to a psychiatrist, who asked him to lie on his couch.

"Now," said the psychiatrist, "what seems to be the trouble?"

"Well," said the man, "I have a terrible problem. I own a large detached house, a cottage in the country, a villa in Spain, a Rolls Royce and a yacht."

"What could possibly be the problem?" asked the psychiatrist.

"I only earn eight pounds a week!"

The vicar was walking along the street when he came across a little girl who was crying.

"What's the matter, my dear?" he asked.

"I haven't got anyone to play with," she sobbed.

"There, there," said the vicar, drying her tears. "I'll play with you. What shall we do?"

"You can start by opening that heavy front gate for me," said the girl with a grin.

"Now what shall I do?" asked the vicar, as they walked up the garden path.

"Ring the doorbell, which is too high for me," said the girl.

"And now what shall I do?" asked the vicar.

"Run like mad!" replied the girl, "before you get caught!!!"

A man went into a bar with jelly and cream in one ear. The barman said to him: "Excuse me sir, do you know you've got jelly and cream in one ear?"
The man replied: "You'll have to speak up, I'm a trifle deaf."

First boy: "I've just had my dog put down."
Second boy: "Was he mad?"
First boy: "He was livid."

First boy: "Every morning I get up at dawn, wake up my dog, and we go for a tramp in the woods."
Second boy: "Isn't the tramp getting a bit fed up with it?"

The vicar caught two small boys smoking. "Do you know where little boys go when they smoke?" he asked them sombrely.

"Yes," replied one. "Behind the bicycle sheds."

A famous mountaineer had a terrible accident. He fell down a ravine, and injured both arms and legs. The rescue team couldn't get a stretcher down to him, so eventually they hit on the only possible rescue plan. Lowering a rope to the injured man, they told him to grip it hard with his teeth, and they would pull him up to safety. All went well until the man was a few metres from the top. At that point one of the rescuers leaned over the edge and asked: "Are you okay?"; and the mountaineer replied: "I'm okaaaaaaaaaaaaaaaaaaaaa . . ."

A man went to have his eyes tested. The optician told him to sit down and look at a board which had some letters written on it.

"Now then," said the optician, "can you read the top letter?"

"No," replied the man.

The optician held it closer.

"Can you read it now?"

"No".

He held it closer still.

"Can you read it now?"

"No," replied the man.

"Goodness," said the optician," this is serious!"

"I know," said the man. "I can't read!"

SIGH!

A plump lady tried on the largest dress in the shop. It didn't fit.

"You'll just have to diet," suggested the assistant politely.

"What colour?" asked the lady.

A man visiting a museum was told by the cloakroom attendant to leave his umbrella in the cloakroom. The man told him he didn't have an umbrella.

"Then you can't come in," said the attendant.

"Why not?" asked the man.

"Because," replied the attendant, "I have orders that people can't come in without leaving umbrellas in the cloakroom."

First man: "I like your new cap."

Second man: "Thanks. I used to wear a pork pie, but the gravy kept running into my ears."

First man: "I've put too many stamps on this letter."

Second man: "I hope it doesn't go too far."

A west country farmer was leaning on the gate to his farm when an American tourist stopped for a chat.

"Cute little farm you got here" the tourist observed. "How big is it?"

"Thirty hectares," replied the farmer.

"Thirty hectares!" exclaimed the tourist. "Why, I've got a farm in Texas which takes me three days to drive around. What do you say to that?"

"I'd say," replied the farmer, after a moment's thought, "that you should get a new car."

A small boy had broken his arm, and the doctor was putting it in plaster.

"Scuse me doc," said the boy. "Will I be able to play the violin when the plaster comes off?"

"I certainly think so, young man," replied the doctor.

"That's amazing!" exclaimed the boy."

"Why should that be so amazing?" asked the doctor.

"Because I've never been able to play it up 'til now!"

35

A man took his dog for a walk in the park. He hadn't gone very far when a crowd gathered to admire his dog which was, to say the least, unusual.

"What's it called?" asked one man.

"It's a long-nosed, long-tailed terrier," answered the man. "And what's more," he added, "it's the fiercest dog in the world."

"Nonsense!" said another man. "My Alsatian would make mincemeat of him!"

On hearing this the long-nosed long-tailed terrier turned, took one look at the Alsatian, and with one bite swallowed it whole!

"He couldn't do that to my Doberman Pinscher!" ventured another man who had seen what had happened. Whereupon the terrier rounded on the Doberman and gulped it down!

"Amazing!" said a third man. "What sort of a dog did you say it is?"

"It's a long-nosed, long-tailed terrier," replied the man. "Mind you," he added, "some people call them alligators."

Every year, on the day of the Queen's birthday, a parcel of big purple plums would arrive at the palace from an address in the west country. This went on for so many years that at last an equerry was sent to investigate.

He arrived at the address and knocked on the door, which was answered by a little old lady.

"Good morning, madam," began the equerry. "I'm from Buckingham Palace. I've been sent to ask you why you always send a parcel of plums to her majesty on her birthday."

"Well," said the little old lady. "It was quite a problem at first choosing a present for someone like her. Then I remembered the National Anthem."

"How can that have been helpful?" asked the equerry.

"You know," replied the lady. "The bit where it tells you to 'send her Victorias'."

First steward: "I've just had a devil of a job getting a little old lady to board a flight to Paris."

Second steward: "Why, was she scared of flying?"

First steward: "No. She wanted to go to Amsterdam!"

A man was given a job as a bus driver. When he reported for work on his first morning he asked where his conductor was.

"You don't have a conductor," replied the inspector. "These are one-man buses."

So the man boarded his bus and drove off, while the inspector went to have a cup of tea. Five minutes later the man telephoned the inspector from the High Street to tell him that he'd had a crash.

"What happened?" asked the inspector.

"How should I know?" replied the man. "I was upstairs collecting fares at the time!"

A small boy and an elderly man boarded a crowded bus and, since there were no empty seats, were forced to stand in the aisle.

"Move farther down the bus please!" called the conductor.

"He's NOT my father," said the boy, indignantly. "He's my grandfather."

A little old lady called the guard on her train and asked: "Does this train stop at Brighton, my man?"

"If it doesn't," replied the guard, "there'll be a heck of a splash!"

Posh Lady: "Driver! Do you stop at the Hilton?"
Bus Driver: "Not on my wages, ma'am."

Why do one-man buses make such terrible music?
Because they don't have a conductor.

8   All at Sea?

What is the untidiest part of a ship?
The officers' mess.

What is the strictest part of a ship?
The stern.

What is the most polite part of a ship?
The bow.

Why couldn't the ship's officers play cards?
Because the captain was standing on the deck.

In which part of a ship is it best to drink?
The port side.

9 Jokes galore

How do you know whether your bank manager has a good head for money?
See if he's got a slot in the back of his head.

What's the definition of a "coup de grace"?
A French lawnmower.

Do you think clumsiness is catching?
No, I think it's dropping.

What's thick and yellow and extremely dangerous?
Shark-infested custard.

What zooms through the water at 50 knots?
A motor pike.

Whats a good name for a Scottish cloak-room attendant?
Angus McCoatup.

What stands on the lawn going "tick, tick, tick"?
A metrognome.

What's a good name for an Indian cloak-room attendant?
Mahatma Coat.

What did Santa Claus say in the garden?
"Hoe, hoe, hoe."

What's yellow, tastes of almonds, and swings from cake to cake?
Tarzipan.

What's the difference between a buffalo and a bison?
You can't wash your hands in a buffalo.

Why did the boy go to sleep in the fireplace?
So he could sleep like a log.

What happens if you drop a piano down a mineshaft?
You get A Flat Minor.

Who has a parrot which shouts "Pieces of Four"?
Short John Silver.

How do you start a flea circus?
From scratch.

What's the definition of "aperitif"?
A Frenchman's dentures.

What's the favourite meal of nuclear scientists?
Fission chips.

What's big and hairy and flies at Mach two?
King Kongcorde.

What's big and red and eats rocks?
A big red rock eater.

Why did the psychiatrist put his wife under the bed?
Because he thought she was a little potty.

Where does Tarzan get his clothes?
At a jungle sale.

What do jellybabies wear on their feet.
Gumboots.

What's big and green with a very long face?
The Incredible Sulk.

How do you get down from an elephant?
You don't. You get down from swans.

What's the difference between an elephant and a letter box?
If you don't know I won't send you to post a letter.

Why can't you buy castor oil in Boots?
Because it would run out of the lace holes.

What's the easiest way to make a bandstand?
Take away their chairs.

What's the best thing to take when you are run down?
The car's number.

Did you hear about the daft Teddy Boy?
He fell off the roof trying to put his drainpipes on.

When is a birthday party like a camping holiday?
When the fun is intense.

Where do they make the best car horns?
Hong King.

What do you send men who are looking for oil?
A "Get well" card.

What goes "clip"?
A one-legged horse.

What goes "boing-scrub"?
A spring cleaner.

What did one mindreader say to the other mindreader?
"Hello, you're fine. How am I?"

Did you hear about the boy who does bird impressions?
He eats worms.

What do you get if you cross Darth Vader with a parrot?
I don't know, but if it says "pretty polly", smile.

What's green, covered in custard, and miserable?
Apple grumble.

Why do witches fly on broomsticks?
Because vacuum cleaners are too noisy.

What do you call it when an orchestra robs a bank?
Robbery with violins.

What do you call a robbery at a fishmonger's?
A smash and crab raid.

Where do policemen live?
Letsby Avenue.

Where do detectives live?
Sherlock Holmes.

Who was the biggest robber in the history of the world?
Atlas, because he held up the whole world.

Why will no one ever steal the river Thames?
Because it has so many locks on it.

Which Mafia boss controls the North Sea?
The Codfather.

What did the policeman say when he came across three deep holes?
"Well, well, well."

What do you say to a blonde policeman?
"It's a fair cop."

What did the bus conductor say to the man with three heads, no arms, and one leg?
"Hello, hello, hello. You look 'armless, Hop on."

Did you hear about the fight at the fish and chip shop last night?
Two cod got battered.

A man in a mask rushed into a bank, pointed his finger at the cashier and said, "This is a muck-up!"
"Don't you mean a stick-up?" asked the cashier.
"No," said the man. "It's a muck-up. I've forgotten my gun."

What do you call a man who breaks into a meat factory?
A hamburglar.

What happened to the burglar who stole a calendar?
He got twelve months.

What did the policeman say to the three angels?
"Halo, halo, halo."

Why did the burglar cut the legs off his bed?
He wanted to lie low for a while.

Which detective has the smartest hairstyle?
Sherlock combs.

Policeman: "What gear were you in at the time of the accident?"
Motorist: "A brown overcoat, if it makes any difference."

Why did the boy throw his watch out of the window?
To see how time flies.

Who makes the best ice cream in Israel?
Walls of Jericho.

How do you decorate a spaceship at Christmas?
With missiletoe.

What is big and grey, and mumbles?
Mumbo jumbo.

What do you give a pig with a sore throat?
Oinkment.

Who is given the sack as soon as he starts work?
A postman.

What is black and whizzes round the office?
A fast bowler.

How do you weigh a whale?
At a whale weigh station.

What is a prickly pear?
Two hedgehogs.

Who loves
ya —
baby

What is bald and wobbles?
Jelly Savalas.

What is red and lies in the gutter?
A dead bus.

What does a cat sleep on?
A caterpillow.

What is a Sandwich man?
A snack for a cannibal.

How do you make a Swiss roll?
Push him off an Alp.

Why are elephants wrinkled?
Ever tried ironing one?

Who hold up trains but are never arrested?
Bridesmaids.

How do you hire a horse?
Put a brick under each leg.

What's green and hairy and wears sunglasses?
A gooseberry on holiday.

What does a vegetarian vampire eat?
Blood oranges.

Who swings through the vines?
Tarzan of the Grapes.

Which bird can lift the heaviest weight?
A crane.

Where does dracula live in America?
The Vampire State Building.

How can you help a deaf fisherman?
Give him a herring aid.

Why did the sales assistant take money from the till?
She thought the change would do her good.

How do elephants climb oak trees?
They sit on an acorn and wait.

How do birds get down from great heights?
By sparrowchute.

What sort of skin makes the best slipper?
A banana skin.

Why do you get punctures?
Forks in the road.

Who look after sick gnomes?
The National Elf Service.

Why is a radio set never complete?
Because it's always a wireless.

What is brown, hairy and bashful?
A coconut shy.

What is round, red and cheeky?
Tomato sauce.

Why is a fishmonger a mean man?
His job makes him sell fish.

Man: "Any dogs going cheap?"
Pet shop owner: "Sorry. Ours go 'woof'!"

Why didn't the skeleton go to the party?
Because he had no body to go with.

What is round and green and barks?
A grape dane.

Who cooks the chips at a monastery?
The friar.

What did the grape say when the elephant trod on it?
Nothing. It just gave a little wine.

What goes "croak-croak" when it's misty?
A froghorn.

Where do you play if you have a rubber trumpet?
In an elastic band.

What carries people under the sea?
An octobus.

What do you call a parrot with a machine gun?
A parrot trooper.

What do you call a flying elephant?
A jumbo jet.

What do you call a boat that lies on the bottom of the sea and shakes?
A nervous wreck.

When is a shop like a yacht?
When it has a sale on.

What sort of fur should you get from a skunk?
As fur as possible.

If a horse wears shoes, what should a camel wear?
Sandals.

What did the beaver say to the tree?
Nice to gnaw you.

What should you do if you swallow fifty pence?
Go to bed and wait for some change.

Why is a cat's milk like a slow racing driver?
Both get lapped.

Why do dustmen never accept invitations?
Because they are refuse men.

Why are onions like bells?
They both peel.

Why do bears have fur coats?
They'd look stupid in anoraks.

What weighs 250,000 tonnes and tastes of tomato?
A soupertanker.

What did the idiot call his pet zebra?
"Spot."

Whats red and runs in slow motion?
The bionic nose.

Why is a nursery like a dance hall?
Both have a bawlroom.

What do short-sighted ghosts wear?
Spooktacles.

What does a Scotsman sleep under?
A continental kilt.

What's made of glass and howls?
A bay window.

Why are the Cossacks the world's fastest horsemen?
Because they are always Russian.

What's covered in safety pins and sleeps two?
A punk bed.

What has three legs and lives at the bottom
of the sea?
A piano tuna.

How do you catch squirrels?
Climb a tree and act like a nut.

How do you catch rabbits?
*Hide behind a bush and make a noise like a
lettuce.*

Where do astronauts park their spaceships?
Parking meteors.

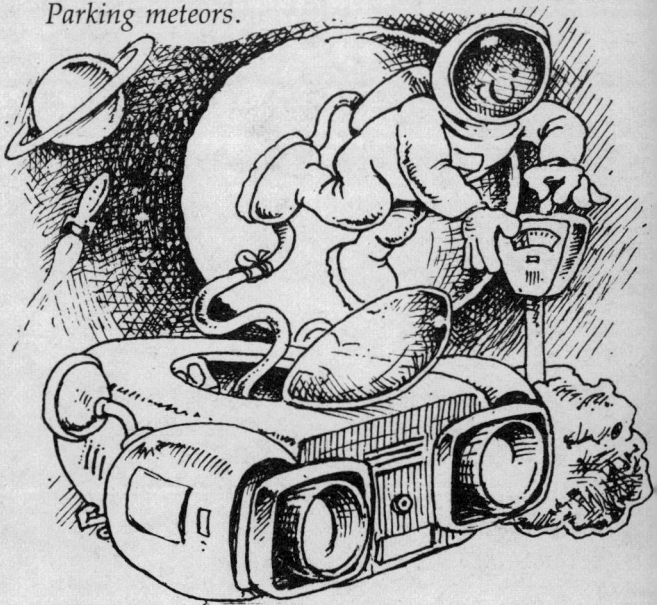

What is a weather forecaster's favourite
game?
Draughts.

10 Medical Matters

SURGERY →

"Doctor, doctor, I keep thinking I'm a pack of cards."
"Sit down and I'll deal with you in a moment."

"Doctor, doctor, people are always ignoring me."
"Next."

"Doctor, doctor, I've lost my voice."
"Now then, what seems to be the trouble?"

"Doctor, doctor, my hair's falling out. Can you give me something to keep it in?"
"What about this paper bag?"

"Doctor, doctor, I'm having trouble remembering things."
"How long has this been going on?"
"How long has what been going on?"

11 Mother, Mother . . .

There's a man at the door dressed like Long John Silver.
Tell him to hop it.

There's a man at the door selling bee hives.
Tell him to buzz off.

There's a man at the door with a bill.
Why hasn't he got a nose like everyone else?

The invisible man's at the door.
Tell him I can't see him.

There's a man at the door with a funny face.
Tell him you've already got one.

There's a man at the door with a drum.
Tell him to beat it.